Chuff is a very big cat.

He has a dish as big as a hat.

It is full of chocolate chips.

Can you see Chuff lick his lips?

Chuff gobbles the chips very quick.

His tum is full.

He feels sick.

So he sits on Kevin's bed.

"I am sick," the big cat said.

Kevin goes to look in his dish.

He sees a chop and a chunk of fish.

He licks his chop.

Yum, yum, yum.

Then he chats to his chum.

But Chuff is looking very sick.

He gobbled the chocolate chips too quick.

"I wish I'd had a chunk of fish,

not chocolate chips,

in my dish."